Learning About Snow

Kathy Smith

Rosen
REAL
READERS

The Rosen Publishing Group, Inc.
New York

Snow falls when it is cold.

Snowflakes are frozen drops
of water.

Snowplows move snow out of the way.

You can make a snowman
with snow.

You can make a house
with snow.

You can go for a ride on
the snow.

Words to Know

snow

snowflakes

snowman

snowplow